*"To become who you want to be,
You must first change your thinking."*
- *Mike Rodriguez*

For Bonnie, who always encourages me to think **BIG**.

THINK

BIG

Motivational Quotes

MIKERODRIGUEZ

Copyright © 2016
Mike Rodriguez International
Frisco, Texas

Tribute Publishing

Think BIG Motivational Quotes
First Edition May 2016

All Worldwide Rights Reserved
ISBN: 978-0-9906001-6-9

All Rights Reserved. No part of this book may be reproduced, stored in a retrieval system, or transmitted, in any form, or by any means, electronic, recorded, photocopied, or otherwise, without the prior written permission of the copyright owner, except by a reviewer who may quote brief passages in a review.

Printed in the United States of America.

Throughout my life and career, I have often relied on words of inspiration from the great ones when I was feeling down, maintaining my attitude or just needing a boost.

The quotes and words shared by the likes of my mentors: Jim Rohn, Tom Hopkins, Bryan Tracy, Og Mandino and others including John Maxwell, Zig Ziglar, Dale Carnegie, etc., helped to shape me into the speaker, trainer and author that I am today.

Early on I realized that if I wanted to become big, I needed to think BIG.

My hope is that my original words contained in *"Think BIG"* can now help you through whatever it is that you are facing. Read them as often as you like or as you need to. Carry this book with you and share the quotes with others. Think BIG and take your life beyond the small.

Let's start thinking BIG!

**"TODAY I will overcome my BIGGEST Challenge.
I am confident
I am ready
I will begin
I WILL WIN!"**

Too many times we put off facing our difficult challenges until tomorrow. Change your thoughts, believe you will win and face them head-on today.

"The only true limitations you will have are those that you accept and believe."

What you accept in your mind is what you will follow. I encourage you to know that you are capable of achieving much more than what you currently believe. Believe you can do more, take BIG action and you will accomplish more.

"Your Direction in life starts with your belief system. What you believe is what you will follow."

Challenge yourself to uncover how you view yourself and what you believe. Are you heading down the right path for your life's calling? What do you believe?

"Where you are in your life right now is only temporary.
It's up to you to let it become permanent."

You may be somewhere physically or even mentally that you do not want to be. If your desire is strong enough, you can change your situation. Keep moving forward and don't stay where you don't want to be!

"Keep away from those who belittle your ambitions."

Sometimes we can easily spot negative people. Other times, we can receive negative influence from those we care about the most. Either way, distance yourself from those who are not helping you to succeed. You deserve more!

> "Act, think and speak for where you expect to be, not for where you are."

You may not be in a job, home, relationship or circumstance that you want or need to be in. That's OK. It's not OK to allow yourself to be pulled down. Always represent yourself well, so you can believe in where you need to be. Make it real, so it will become real!

"Believing in who you already are is the starting point to becoming who you want to be?"

You are made with a purpose. You have unique skills, desires and talents. You must embrace yourself and love who you are before you can become more.

"Improve your chances for success. Don't try…COMMIT!"

Anything worthwhile is difficult and will require BIG efforts! BIG efforts will only come with commitment. When you commit to something your mind locks in and starts looking for more ways to succeed. If you simply try, you will get less that you deserve. Don't try, DO IT!

> **"Success is a series of steps taken one at a time. You will slow, you will stop and you will go backwards, but you must always keep moving forward."**

When you have BIG dreams they can seem overwhelming. However, when you take small steps, you can control your direction and accomplish a little bit each day. These little steps are the building blocks to BIG success.

> "Success starts
> when your actions become
> **BIGGER** than your
> excuses."

Stop telling yourself why you can't. Stop believing why you can't. Stop making excuses and Start putting BIG Actions into motion. You will start to realize success!

"Failure is a result of what you did, not of who you are."

If you do something and fail, YOU are not a failure. You simply experienced failure. Use it as a learning experience and keep going until you succeed!

"To change your world, start changing your life."

I hear people say that they want a better life. I hear people say that their world is falling apart. Your world is turned by your life. Live your life the way you should and your world will follow.

"People and decisions can change your life. Make sure you have great ones in yours."

Make sure that every person and every decision in your life is helping you to get closer to living your best life. Represent yourself well by being with great people and by making great decisions.

"Sometimes it's not about what you see, it's how you choose to see it."

When you face difficulties, you can view them as obstacles, as the end, or as an opportunity. It's always YOUR choice.

"Those who aren't seeking treasure won't follow any map given to them."

Don't try to convince people to change. Don't try to convince people to follow their dreams. Help them to uncover their own potential so they can convince themselves to take action on their own.

"Change your thoughts, actions and words; change your life."

These are the three things that YOU can always control. If you want or need a better quality of life, start here.

"When the pain of your current situation becomes greater than the pain of change, that's when it is time to change."

Everyone wants to change something. Create your own motivation and incentive to overcome what is holding you back. Experience the pain of change for a little while, so you can experience the benefits of success for a lifetime.

"Whatever you think is impossible, will become impossible."

If you have accepted that something cannot or will not happen, it won't. You won't let it. Believe in you, believe in the possibilities and take action!

"Today is a new day and it is yours."

Today is not yesterday, as yesterday is gone. Tomorrow isn't here yet. What will you do with your new day full of opportunity?

"YOU are responsible for making your life great."

Don't rely on or expect anyone else to create your life. It is your life. Own it, plan it, love it and live in a way that honors who you are.

"Any change in your life starts with a decision."

Yes, change is difficult, but not impossible. The reality is that all difficult change must first start with a simple decision.

"Life's challenges are meant to **REFINE** us, not to **DEFINE** us."

You will face problems, difficulties and challenges in your life. These things do not define who you are. They should help you to refine who you are becoming.

"Failure is an opportunity to re-evaluate."

If you take action and face failure, don't worry, this is a good thing. You now have an opportunity to re-evaluate your next move.

"When you find your PASSION, you release your confidence!"

Are you lacking in your career or life situation? Discover what you are passionate about and your confidence will soar!

"Who are YOU becoming?"

Your thoughts, words and actions are the building blocks of who you are. Are you proud of those things? If not, take action to change them.

"You must break your routines to fix your life."

If something in your life is holding you back and keeping you from your potential, you must change your routines. Just because you are comfortable doing something, doesn't mean that it is effective for your life.

"When others say YOU Can't, It just tells me that they believe THEY Can't!"

When you pursue your goals you will find that other people who have failed, sometimes want to discourage you from even starting. That is their journey, you have your own and you will have different results!

"Today is all I have, so I'll start today."

Too many times we procrastinate and wait for tomorrow, next week or even next year. Today is the best day to start. It is here and it is all that you have right now. Make it BIG!

"As long as you are breathing, your life has value."

At times, we can feel useless. This is a false and destructive feeling. Remember who you are and whose you are. The breath in your lungs is a reminder that you have value and you still have work to do. Get started.

"How will **YOU** be remembered?"

Every situation that you are in is an opportunity to improve your life and create value for others. Do the things that impact the lives of others and they will not forget.

"Having a weakness does not mean that YOU are weak."

None of us are perfect and we should not strive for perfection. Likewise, all have flaws and weaknesses. Always work to strengthen yourself. You should strive for excellence.

"Smiles create smiles. Share yours."

One of the most contagious acts that can be spread across many people, regardless of language barriers, is to smile.

> "See yourself as
> **STRONG,** not weak
> **BRAVE,** not afraid
> **PEACEFUL,** not worried
> **HAPPY,** not sad
> And eventually
> you **WILL BE.**"

How you choose to see yourself and what you choose to believe about yourself, are the building blocks to who you will become.

"Have faith."

Living a life without faith is like walking in the dark. Know and believe that you CAN and that things WILL happen, in their due time.

"Appreciate where you are. It's preparing you for where you are going."

If you don't like your situation, don't give up. You don't have to like it, but you must go through it. All things serve a higher purpose. Think BIG!

> **"You have the ability to change your mindset about who you are and what you are going to do about your life."**

Are you unhappy about something in your life? Make a decision to change it and start today. It is your life, own it!

"Don't TELL others who you are. Show them!"

Words are great. Actions are even better. It's easy to talk and more difficult to take action. When you take action, others will take notice and you will benefit!

"You can overcome all that you believe you can overcome."

When you face a challenge and you don't think you can go through it, you won't. Step into your greatness, believe in you and your capabilities and take action.

"There is never a point where your life is ruined. Become stronger and keep going!"

One of the worst things that you can do to yourself is to believe that a mistake you made, defines you. Everyone makes mistakes. Mistakes are a learning experience of what you DID, not who you ARE. Own it and move on.

"You must get to the point where the passion to pursue your goals, drowns your fears."

What goals and dreams have you been holding out on? Starting today, forget your excuses, remember your passion and get to work!

"Eliminate excuses, create solutions."

It's easy to come up with reasons why you can't. You might even believe them. Challenge yourself to come up with ways to think positive.

"Write a NEW future, let go of your past."

Your current situation is a result of your past decisions and experiences. When you start changing, you create new experiences and new memories.

"Limiting your potential to make others feel better, cheats everyone."

Don't limit yourself to make others feel better. Do your best and challenge them to rise to their potential.

"Leaders talk facts, followers spread opinions."

If you are spreading your opinions, it's all about what YOU think. Share facts and welcome input to learn and grow.

"You must believe in yourself, if you expect anyone else to."

People might love you and care about you, but no one will follow you and invest in you if you don't show that you are worthy and capable.

"If you want better results, YOU must become better."

Nothing in your life will start to change until you change. Your life is a reflection of what you choose to do.

> "Build your dreams with purposeful action and destroy your excuses."

When you start working towards your dreams, you will, in fact, eliminate your excuses. Your actions will build your confidence.

"Change YOU and everything else will start to change."

Once you start to change, you will see that your attitude causes you to change how you think, act and speak. People around you will respond.

"YOUR LIFE:
Are you hanging around?
or
Are you climbing?"

Quit talking and thinking about your goals. You must take action and work hard to make your dreams come true.

"Some will confuse your confidence with arrogance, know who you are."

People who don't understand your belief and your passion for your dreams, confuse that positive force with arrogance. As long as you know and live with humble respect, you will be OK.

"Confidence begins with knowing who you are."

You should strive to be confident. You should start believing in yourself by appreciating who you are, knowing your gifts and respecting yourself.

"Courage is already inside of you. Use it and it will grow to meet your challenge."

When you are confronted with your deepest fears and your biggest challenges, your courage will be ready to use, if you call on it.

> **"Don't wait for a major event to start making changes in your life, create the event."**

Most of us are waiting for the perfect time to start or we will start when something bad happens. Don't wait! Make your own situation and start today.

> "Ready to make an impact on your life?
> Decide and take action."

You can start changing when you recognize the need. First, make a decision and then do something.

"Never let someone else determine your destiny."

Others may have big ideas for your life or little ideas. Follow your own calling. It's your life.

"Your routines must change if you want to change."

What you are doing each day determines who you are becoming. Change what you are doing and you can become more.

"Regret is baggage you don't want to carry around. Let it go."

You can live with being tired and you can live with working hard. Both build you up like muscles. Regrets are like weights on your mind, morale, confidence and purpose.

"When you train with champions, you can win championships."

Who you learn from influences your strategy, philosophy and determination. Be around and learn from those that are improving and succeeding.

"Be careful with your thoughts. You will inevitably find what your mind is looking for."

When you look for ugly things you will find them. When you look for the good in things in life (and people) you will find them. Always be aware of your mindset.

"NO ONE has the power to make you feel bad. Your power, your choice."

It's your brain, your thoughts and your emotions. People can say hurtful or mean things, but that doesn't mean you have to hurt. Be strong and think positive.

"When we fail to execute, we are destined to fail."

If you want to succeed, but you don't want to work, you won't take action. No action means no results.

"You will eventually become like the people you choose to associate with. Who can you afford to be around and for how long?"

Be very aware of your close friends. Nice people who are negative or who do bad or immoral things can ruin your life. Smile, keep your distance and move on.

"You must learn from everything, to become something."

In good times and bad, through success and failures, always ask yourself what you learned, then really apply it. This is how you become the best you.

> **"Know who you are,
> so you won't become
> something else."**

No one can tell you that you are less
than you are if you know who you are.
Believe in and appreciate yourself.

"Saying I WILL, always gets better results than saying I'll try."

When you make a commitment, not only do you feel it, but others believe more. Your mind will cause you to work harder.

> "If you think you can't,
> you won't.
> Change your thoughts,
> Change your life."

Your mind is powerful. If you don't believe it, you won't do it. Find out why you doubt and then make change!

"Are you being held down by fear or being Lifted by faith?"

Fear is based on thoughts in your own mind. They make you trap yourself. Have faith in what you cannot see, be happy and confident and take action.

"Your past is only an issue, If you still live there."

If you made mistakes and you are still living with them, that is your own problem. No one is making you re-live or carry your mistakes. Let them go.

> **"Push yourself beyond what you can imagine and things will start to happen."**

Since your body will only push you to what you believe; believe more and push farther. You will realize you can accomplish more.

"Your own voice will be the strongest influence in your own life. Make it count."

Don't listen to negative words others have to say. Start pumping yourself up by putting great stuff in your mind! You will believe everything you tell yourself!

"Don't be your biggest obstacle."

If you are thinking, doing, or saying things that prevent you from being your best, you are being your biggest obstacle.

"Act, think and speak for where you expect to be, not for where you are."

Do you want to be a leader, a better parent or a better person? Start acting like one. You may not be there now, but believe that you are and you will start to become.

> "Each day, do a little bit more and you will start to become a little bit better."

The changes you need to make today, need to begin today. Do a little bit more, believe a little bit more, and these small steps will conquer BIG stairways.

> "You must tell yourself
> **I CAN,**
> Even when you think
> you can't."

You are becoming what you think about. Change your actions by changing your thoughts. Continually tell yourself that you can and that you are capable.

"Pursuing your dreams is hard. It's OK to accept that. It's never OK to give up on your dreams because it's too hard."

Giving up is always the easy way out. Your passion for your dreams will keep you going. It will pay off in the end.

"There are many obstacles that will keep you from reaching your goals. You believing them will be the biggest."

Nothing in your life will hold you back as much as you believing that you can no longer go on. It's a lie. Don't believe it.

"You must work daily to keep the weeds out of your life and mind."

Negative thoughts, fear and doubt are a few of the weeds that you must fight each day. Fertilize your mind and life with positivity and powerful words!

"Failure is just an opportunity to re-evaluate."

When you face failure, be proud and announce that you just found a way that doesn't work. Now it's time to learn why, adjust and keep going.

"NEVER negotiate with mediocrity."

When you settle for less, you will get less, but you will start going downhill a little bit at a time. Take the challenge and go BIG!

> "Some show up because they have to.
> Most show up and do the work.
> Few show up to win."

Some haven't found their purpose yet; others live in negativity or they are just lost. Not you. You will do more and become more.

"You cannot overcome what you will not face."

All problems are temporary. Face them head on, go through them and you will conquer them. Maybe not the way you want to, but you will become stronger as a result.

"When you complain about your problems, you are empowering them."

Everyone has problems and everyone faces challenges. Don't complain about them. You are keeping the issue in your mind without any resolution. Think of solutions and own them!

"Find your strength and others will follow."

When you know who you are and what you are capable of, you are creating a vision. Others can then see it and will believe in you and what you are doing.

"You were designed not by chance, but by choice. Your birth was a miracle and your creation is a testament that you are called to this world to serve a higher purpose."

The only mistakes in life are the ones we make. You are a miracle, given all the tools that you need to succeed. Learn from your mistakes, become better and pursue your purpose!

> "Change is uncomfortable. Choose to be uncomfortable for a while, so you can change your results for a lifetime."

When you feel the need to change, find your courage. You can do it and you will make it through the temporary pain. Enjoy the benefits for the rest of your life.

"YOU are the CEO your own life. Where are you taking You?"

You are in charge of the decisions in your life. You may not be where you want to be, but you can change if you just give the command.

**"When you start believing more and start doing more,
you will start becoming more."**

In order to become more, you must start doing more. Word harder and think bigger. In order to achieve that, you must believe beyond what you can imagine. Have faith in God's plan for your life.

"If you introduced a bad habit, person or situation in your life, then you can remove it."

You weren't designed with flaws; you were designed to live and succeed. If you have created flaws through bad choices, you must change them and start fresh.

"Focus on what you can do and get it done."

Don't be overwhelmed by all of life's issues. Decide what you can handle first, do it and then move on to the next matter. As you accomplish tasks, you will build your confidence!

> **"Success will mean something different to everyone. Know what success means to you."**

Success is a personal thing. It's not about money, wealth or material possessions. Don't let someone else define success for you based on what they think. Wealth will come when you find your success.

"You have already been prepared to overcome what stands ahead of you. Have faith."

God has given you all that you need to succeed. He has prepared your path and set the trail in your favor. It may not be the path you want to take, but it is the right way for his results.

"Your life wasn't meant to be small. Live it in a BIG WAY."

Don't settle for less than you can become. Your talents and passions are unique to you. Believe in yourself and start making BIG changes.

"Change YOU, Change your life."

If your life isn't what you expected, that's okay. Start changing you and the rest of your life will follow.

"Pay less attention to the words people use, and more attention to why they are using them."

Sometimes people say words that don't accurately describe what they are thinking. Don't get caught up in the words, think beyond to the core of the person.

**"Know your value.
Never let anyone decide
for you."**

Someone may have told you or maybe they are still telling you who you are. They are wrong if it isn't building you up. Don't listen to them. Change what you do and change the facts.

"Your life will only become as **BIG** as you believe."

Your life plan has been established and God will create the way. Don't put limits on yourself and don't let any person put limits on you. Believe BIG and take BIG action.

"Life will seem easier when you become stronger."

If you are facing difficulties today, that's okay. You are stronger inside and can do more if you own it and accept it. Become stronger and you can manage through life.

"When you stop saying the word *can't,* you remove your first obstacle."

The word can't is only based on a belief system. Either from someone else or from your own mind. Don't say "Can't." Say "I CAN." Then take action and keep going. You might fail temporarily, but keep going until you succeed.

"Remember that criticism, negativity and spitefulness are only reflections of the person giving them. You don't have to accept them."

When you hear negativity from certain people, know that it isn't about you. They are jealous or threatened and are simply sharing their feelings with you. They want you to own those feelings to feel like they do. Don't accept them.

"Your life has value and a purpose. As long as you are breathing, you have a responsibility to respect your value and to discover your purpose."

Never give up. Accept that the breath in your lungs is proof that you should be alive. Use that breath to take action and put your talents to work to change lives, starting with your own.

"When you find your strength you will find a way."

Weakness creates confusion and doubt. These feelings are temporary and can be overcome. Know who you are, think BIG and you will become stronger.

"You cannot become great with a mediocre attitude."

BIG results require BIG thinking. When you think BIG, your attitude follows.

"Excuses are life's anchors. What's holding you down?"

You will always find an excuse if you are looking for one. They are easy to find. The problem starts when you believe them and you convince yourself and others why you can't.

"People who don't want to change, don't want you to change."

When you choose to change, it will make others uncomfortable. They will work to get you to stay at the same level they are. Stay strong and move on.

"Don't give up. It might be about to happen."

Too many times I see people who have decided to make a change. Too many times I see them quit before their actions can pay off. Stay the course!

> **"Starting today
> DECIDE who you are,
> FIND your strength,
> BELIEVE in yourself
> And NEVER give up."**

When you choose to accept your greatness, you will become stronger with every positive word you say and every step you take. Keep going!

"Align yourself with the Doers, not the Talkers."

Many people like to talk about who they are and what they are going to do, but they never do anything; they are the talkers. Be the one who takes action and hang with those who take action.

> **"People with a true purpose never give up. They rise to face another day, even when they are temporarily defeated."**

When you know who you are and what you are living for, you know that setbacks are all temporary. You will lose and you will fall. Get back up to win again another day.

"Every broken life can be rebuilt."

You weren't made or born broken. You were created by divine design. If your life isn't right or where you need to be, trust in the great healer to make the necessary repairs. God is always with you and will never leave you. Decide today to start new.

"DO and you might. DON'T and you won't."

Too many times I hear people tell others that they can't do something. Don't listen. Remember that if you don't get started it will never happen. Take action and you will have a chance!

> **"NEVER convince yourself it's over. While you are still alive, you still have a chance."**

A defeat or a loss in life is never good, but can be overcome. God is on your side. He will give you the strength you need. Use your breath as his promise and commitment to your life. He has given it to you to breathe, act and live.

"Your presence in this world is proof of your purpose."

Many people are looking for their purpose. It's not on the outside. It's what God has put inside you. Accept him into your life and supercharge your purpose!

"You will move in the directions of your thoughts. Where are you taking yourself?"

What you think about, your mind will follow. It is like a finely tuned GPS. Put good stuff in and you will go to BIG places!

"It's never too late to change your mind about changing your direction."

Did you make a bad decision? Are you going down a wrong path? It's not too late for you. Simply turn around, RUN and don't look back. It's your life, make a new decision. Own it!

"When you give into your fears, you empower them. Stay strong."

Your fears are created through your personal thoughts. The more you think about your fears the more you feed them. Starve them by claiming success.

"YOU are responsible for making your life GREAT!"

You can get caught up living each day doing the same stuff, without making progress, waiting for something to happen. Don't wait, take BIG action to get BIG results!

"Wait for everything to be perfect and you will keep waiting."

When you have an idea or dream that pulls at you, you need to pursue it if it is for good purposes. Don't wait for the perfect time, God will make your path perfect.

"*It can't be done.* Is only said by the weak."

People who say it can't be done, say that because they don't believe they can do it. Don't listen to them.

> "Those who **DO** usually get the most criticism from those Who **CAN'T** or **WON'T**."

When you take action to pursue your dreams, it makes others who didn't take action feel uncomfortable. Don't let their negativity slow you down.

> "My failures don't define me. They are a reminder of my passion to succeed."

When you fail, YOU are NOT a failure. You need to remember what you are doing, learn from your mistake and become stronger!

> "Believe that there is more.
> Know that there is a way.
> Find your strength."

Trouble and problems create doubt. Don't let it enter your mind. Know who you are and whose you are. God is on your side.

"Your future is waiting for you.
Start the journey."

You have the opportunity to put your skills, talents and desires to work. There is a catch; you must get started!

"Knowing what to do means absolutely nothing, If you don't do it.

Too many people read too much stuff but never do anything with it. Knowledge left to thought will fade.

"Some things require too much effort to hold on to. Know when to let go."

If you are holding on to something that isn't good for you or that keeps pulling you away, you must let go. Stay with those people and things that bring value to you.

"Your level of effort determines your level of success."

Are you getting mediocre results, or are you failing? It's time to step it up. What you put in, you will get out. When you do more you will become more.

> "Lift yourself above your fears. Rise and meet Your challenges."

Fear can be paralyzing. Don't give in to it. Change your thoughts, think BIG, act BIG and overcome what you are facing.

"Which list is longer, Your excuses or your goals?"

Be honest with yourself and quit believing all of your excuses. Make a goal list that is BIG enough to drown your excuses.

"Those who are down, want to bring you down. Stay strong and look up."

People who are unhappy want you with them. Know who you are, stay strong and look up for your strength.

"Your biggest mistake is holding on to your past mistakes."

Everybody makes mistakes. You don't have to make them a part of your life. Let go of your past and you will be free.

"Use the words from your critics to push you to new heights."

When people tell you that you can't do something, or when they say bad things about you, use that hot air to push you to new levels!

"When you overcome your obstacles, you gain power."

It is easy to feel weak when you face a problem. Remember who is with you and remember that once you face it and go through it, you will become stronger.

> "When you face an obstacle, find a new way. Don't give up."

An obstacle is an opportunity to become stronger and test your resourcefulness.

"Don't let the negative opinions of others influence your decisions."

When negative people run their mouths, nothing good will happen. Make your own decision based on your talents, opportunities and your faith in God.

"Make plans, not excuses."

Excuses are the easy way out, but will create complications for you. Think BIG and create a plan instead.

> "Just beyond what you think is impossible, you will find your greatest success."

Many times the end part of the journey will start to generate the greatest rewards.

"If you keep waiting to take action on your goals, you will gain something…. REGRET."

Enough said. Believe it and get started.

"Your results will get better when YOU become better."

If you aren't getting the results you need, start becoming capable of delivering better results. Read, learn, train and grow.

**"Success is about doing what others are not willing to do. Some will ignore you, some will criticize you, few will join you.
Just keep going."**

It will seem odd to others when you pursue BIG goals. It's not necessary for them to understand you. Move on.

"Success is the great equalizer. It displays your confidence and strengths while exposing your critic's insecurities and weaknesses."

Leave the revenge to the Lord. Your actions and attitude, when managed through faith, will create success for you.

"The only thing worse than failing to take action is having a bad attitude."

If you aren't going to take action now, then make sure you are keeping your attitude in line. Stay focused and prepare to win!

"You cannot build a skyscraper with a shovel. You cannot become a **BIG** success with a small mindset."

BIG goals require a BIG mindset, BIG skills and BIG action. Believe and make it happen!

"It's not your employer's responsibility to train you to become better.
It's yours."

You will have many employers. Your employer is a resource to earn money and gain experience. You are the CEO of your own life and must develop yourself personally.

"Win in your mind and you will start to win in life."

Picture success in your mind. Believe it, feel it and taste it. What you see as real you will make real.

"Carrying baggage from your past will hold you back. Empower yourself, let it go and move forward."

Your past is a lesson to learn from. Use it to gain new insight. Your past is what you did, not who you are.

**"If you change
your surroundings,
but not yourself,
everything will eventually
become the same."**

You can change jobs, homes, locations and relationships, but if you don't change, nothing will ever really change.

"Remove your limits and your results will follow."

Your limits are holding you back. Figure out why you have them, remove them, and go BIG!

"Today is your opportunity to take action on what you dreamed about yesterday."

Don't wait for tomorrow. If you are called to do something today, then act today! God is talking to you!

> **"In life, you will get tired. Tired of making excuses or tired from working towards your dreams."**

You must pay a price in life. Decide what you are willing to live with. See yourself living your dreams.

"Making any change in your life simply starts with making a decision."

Ready to make a BIG change? First, you must make a little decision. Next, you must plan and then take BIG action.

"Know who is influencing your life.
Know when to make changes."

I see too many people who are being held back by people they love. Your life is too important to let someone else hold you back. God has BIG plans for you.

"Do not carry failures and mistakes from your past. You must let them go. You cannot change your past, but you can accept your past, forgive yourself and you can write a new future if you choose to."

"*Dream*
without limits,
Believe
without doubt,
Act
without fear."

Now go forth and make
YOUR LIFE Exceptional!

Start today….

About the Author

Mike Rodriguez is CEO of Mike Rodriguez International, a professional speaking, training and consulting firm. Besides being a Best-Selling author, Mike is a world-renowned motivator and a leadership and sales expert. Mike is also a former showcase speaker with the world famous Zig Ziglar Corporation and was selected as their speaker for the 2015 Ziglar U.S. Tour.

Mike delivers performance-based seminars and trainings and has authored several books which have been promoted by Barnes & Noble. He has been featured on CBS, U.S. News and World Report and has lectured at Baylor University, UNT and K-State Research. His clients include names like Hilton, the Federal Government and McDonald's Corporation.

As a master trainer, Mike has helped thousands.

Everyone faces challenges; Mike believes that through faith and action, you can overcome the challenges in your life to attain your goals and become who you truly want to be.

He is a high-energy leader who worked in corporate America for over two decades training, building, mentoring, and developing top performing people and teams. Mike started as a struggling sales representative, with no experience or formal training. He worked his way up to become a top-performer and an award-winning sales leader. He has held a variety of leadership positions including previously being President & Founder of his own company as a business partner with Southwestern Bell (now AT&T).

As a world-renowned speaker, motivator and master trainer, Mike has experience working with people from all industries.

You can schedule Mike Rodriguez to speak or train at your next event. Go to:
www.MikeRodriguezInternational.com

Other books available by Mike Rodriguez:

Finding Your WHY
8 Keys to Exceptional Selling
Break Your Routines to Fix Your Life
Lion Leadership

Disclaimer & Copyright Information

The author and publisher have made every effort to ensure that the information in this book was correct at press time, the author and publisher do not assume and hereby disclaim any liability to any party for any loss, damage, or disruption caused by errors or omissions, whether such errors or omissions result from negligence, accident, or any other cause.

All quotes, unless otherwise noted, are attributed to the Author.
Cover illustration, book design and production

Copyright © 2016 by Mike Rodriguez International
www.TributePublishing.com

"Go Forth and Make Your Life Exceptional" ™
is a copyrighted trademark of the Author, Mike Rodriguez

NOTES

NOTES

www.ingramcontent.com/pod-product-compliance
Lightning Source LLC
Chambersburg PA
CBHW020616300426
44113CB00007B/660